# When Less than Perfect Is Enough

# When Less than Perfect Is Enough

Poems by

Patricia Horn O'Brien

To Mary Beth
With love &
gratitude for so many
fond memories!

Antrim House
Simsbury, Connecticut

Love,
Pat

Library of Congress Control Number: 2012910629

ISBN: 978-1-936482-26-9

Printed and bound by United Graphics, Inc.

First Edition, 2012

Book design by Rennie McQuilkin

Photographs on cover and pp. iii, 1, 37, and 57 are by the author

Author photograph by Robert Lorenz

Antrim House
860.217.0023
AntrimHouse@comcast.net
www.AntrimHouseBooks.com
21 Goodrich Road, Simsbury, CT 06070

*This book owes a great deal to my mother, father and brother, whose heart-felt attempts to keep us gathered together as a workable family, gave me, without any of us knowing it, what I needed to get by. Their love of life's richness—its friendships, its funny side, its libations, its good books, its ironies, its loyalties, its mysteries and our place in them—has helped me discover the gift in every aspect of my life, whether cheery or not.*

# Acknowledgments

Poems in this collection have also appeared in *Poet Lore, Pulp Smith, Connecticut River Review, Embers, Bean Feast, Fresh Water,* and *Caduceus*.

Thanks to my immediate and extended family and to my good friends, in and out of poetry circles, who have cheered on my poetry pursuits with good nature and infinite patience. And thanks to those mentors and teachers who have broadened my world, in particular my appreciation of literature and poetry, and who have given me the courage and the tools to pursue my writing.

And finally, thanks to Rennie McQuilkin, my editor and publisher, who found value in my work, uncovered its underlying themes, and established an order that gives this book its rhythm and purpose, start to finish.

# Table of Contents

## EPIGRAPH



## I. A BEGINNING



## II. RETRACING

## III. TESTIMONY



## IV. BREAKING NEWS

## *Right Now*

*Happiness is what I want*
*to tell you about.*
*The getting and having,*
*the measuring.*

*Here:*
*live in the same place for five years,*
*watch the cars on the road,*
*wash your dishes in the morning*
*and try to see*
*you will never get another chance*
*to be all-knowing, powerful, and wise.*

*Living won't always make you happy*
*but when you are*
*you'll know why.*

Richard Tietjen
(2/2/1952 – 4/20/2009)

A BEGINNING

## Musings on a Question

*If God exists, what question would you ask?*

I

What exactly is the note that drills a small hole
in my reservoir of tears? Never prepared,
I'm no match for the surprise of it, my throat
inadequate to hold just what
the note's unleashed universe reveals.

II

Have you met my mother, the insomniac
from 2200 Pelham Rd., Apt 4A? On sleepless
nights she'd watch the clicking numbers
on her digital clock. 11:11 was her
favorite time and I have realized
that number, which catches me now
in brief memorials to the hurly-
burly of her days, goes off forever
and forever comes back, an eternity
aglow on her bedside stand.

III

Are you holding my thoughts? They keep
slipping past my days, leaving me in this
ephemeral present which hardly seems

to exist at all! I realize my experience
might pale in the vastness of the universe.
But come on … if anyone can do it …

IV

Who is responsible for the lighting
in this hotel bathroom? Here, before
the mirror, I am at once Messenger and
Her Majesty. What then
is the punishment for shooting
the Messenger?

V

Why am I the one
with flannel sheets and
the *ch-ch-ping-ping-ch*
of radiator heat on those
moonless nights winter
howls through the tiny crack
I've opened my window?
Blankets pulled up to my nose,
I invite in the cold somewhere killing
someone or another.

VI

Maybe you can do the math?
My brother, Mike, age 37, in a head-on crash

in Boca Raton, November 14, 1979,
sparked heaven and earth with his fiery mistake.
His star somewhere in the firmament
rearranged galaxies. I knew he could
do it. But then I hadn't considered
the traveling distance, the speed
of light no match for the weight
of sorrow—for the total weight
of what had never been said.

VII

Is it a mistake to start out
thinking there's a poem in the walk?

Despite the incessant drone of waves
beyond the low tide flats, despite

December's chill slap, words noisier
than winter's gale divide the poet from what

she'd hoped to snare. The lowering sun
surrenders nothing to the moon

in that moment before sleep or dream.
Words for it fill her head.

But what of the gull adrift
on the foam, so recently dead

flight still wafts from his undulating wings—
What?

VIII

Would you eat the pretty bird?
Someone has to.

IX

If nothing has intrinsic meaning
(which I believe is the case) what
meaning sums up the meaning-
lessness?
(I'm keeping my answer
to myself.)

X

So, would you agree irony
is  the overriding category
for all that is meaningless?
(I couldn't resist.)  There is
the risk, of course, of shutting
out sadness and grief
with their attendant
openheartedness.
Cleverness demands
so much distance.

XI

How is it I'm thrilled to hear a remake
of *Bonnie and Clyde* is about to appear?

With four cameras rolling, the two, riddled
with righteous bullets, ricochet between heaven
and this tawdry earth, leaving their force
for us to reckon with.

## XII

Has my dad come around?
Les Horn, who held up the back
of St. Raymond's Church,
East Tremont Ave., the Bronx
on Sunday mornings until he could
no longer bear the weight of it
and, trusting the holy walls
to themselves, sneaked outside
for a cigarette? Mass was ended
at Daly's Bar and Grill, wine
transubstantiated into
so much more, my father's smoke
rising like a heavenly chorus.

## XIII

The video clip soundlessly records
their boots ascending the military
transport steps in the pre-dawn dark,
backlit, it seems,
by a dozen searching moons,
box toe and corrugated sole, foot after
foot: rise fall rise fall.
Their attendant boys and girls
focus only on each step ahead.

Who stands behind those moons
to watch these boots ascend?
Who will await their return,
their silent descent?
Who will count the difference?

## XIV

Can it be that the anthropologist
who, on her latest quest, took
a job on a garbage truck to check
just what signals our trash
sends out, is right? She says
we hate to dwell on our trash
with its inevitable reminder
of our own ephemeral selves.
The carcass plucked. The pit.
The pith. The soggy crusts.
Perhaps they're us. Yes?

Or put another way:
the petal fluttering
from its flower,
the arrow shot,
the waterfall's one
sparkling, flying, diving
drop?

*    *    *

*With each step questions*
*dissipate until, half way*
*across the bridge,*
*I am only my feet,*
*the low slung sun,*
*its watery twin,*
*my beret snug*
*against the wind.*

RETRACING

## Grandfather's Girl

From the low vantage
of my sled I watch the trudging
of your legs, the rise of snow
inside the boots you've cavalierly
left unhooked.  And wrapped around
the red, red roses of your ungloved hands,
the taut, ice-tempered line you use
to pull me close behind.

## Retracing

*for my Grandfather*

Of the few memories not claimed
by childhood's end, the Berkshire calendar remains.
Twelve tear-off pages of days stapled beneath
one black and white photo arrived by mail
each year, compliments of New England Telephone.

Flattened on our enamel table,
pole-studded mountains thinned the still air
of our Bronx apartment. We had to catch our breath
and squint into a sun exploded by the topmost pole.

Down noon-dark declines, the sun's last light spilled,
outlining the spiny poles, the voices
the silent wires hid.

So that was where you worked! With hip-slung tools
and steel-toed shoes, you must have owned
those Massachusetts mountains.

I don't remember what year the calendar stopped.

Oh, the mountains claimed you all right, but not by any
unexpected fault, a casual yawn heaving trees,
swallowing fauna and linemen. Not by an Arctic wind,
yanking your cleats from their perch, ungloving
your strong man's grip.

I would have remembered that.

Instead, you must have climbed down, rung
after rung, signed in your cleats and gloves.
Had someone drive you home.  And in a month,
or years of months, let someone lay you down
in the foothills just outside of town.

## A Study in Family Structure

*Father*: Curved as space
with no edge to lean upon
still I leaned/fell into his spineless center
full of booze and blarney
about warm hearts of the drinking class.
Once he stood tall by me in a sand box,
kept track of his princess in picture albums
where he wrote in white ink
his love.
Once he wrote memoranda that moved the world:
"In regard to this case the law clearly indicates..."
My love
was his then for no asking until,
drunk all the time,
he collapsed inside his armor.
Twenty years ago I mourned him
although he died this spring.

*Mother*: Slippery glass mountain of a woman
with love for no woman—
I hug myself to think of her
(no mother-me-do songs between us,
no sweet tunes).
I do not know her touch unless
you count her shadow cast
across me cool and ever lengthening,
her gentle lighted slopes
reserved for the men of the house.

*Brother*: So I—because he
can hide his real identity, his shape—
will call him him *Mandrake,*
golden boy who makes our mother sing
then *puff!* a snake to make her cry
and blow our father to green fire
doused from bottle to bottle.
True, when he entered on my turf
I played dead to bring him death,
laughed like a witch from unmarked closets
to hear him scream "Momma!"
But I snuggled too with him in bed,
read stories about Jesus until we slept.
Now I hear from his wife he never sleeps
at home, drinks all the time,
angry, exploding his armor.
I feel the tremors in my house,
cry like a damsel in distress.

*I*: Although I am a woman now
I draw my shape from their perimeters,
their weight pulled over me for warmth.
They give me light when they remember
I am here, their moon
eclipsed whole seasons at a time.

## Threshold

He never took my hand on the way home
to ask me to please, please lie for him
about the hours we'd spent at Daly's Bar
and Grill. Besides, I'd liked being propped
on the tall, backless stools, my feet

barely reaching the shiny footrests.
Barely able to swirl right to left. Left
to right. Barely able to raise my elbows
onto the bar's certain curve.

He didn't see the need to ask if I could name
just what he drank. He'd guessed I'd neither
count nor judge the contents of the drinks
so jovially shoved toward where he sat
next to me, his kid.

Besides, I liked the smoke
and the sun's vague passage across
the hot Bronx day while we remained
in the steal-away of Daly's half light.

We were all right until he pressed
the bell of our apartment door and my mother
surveyed us standing in the hall. Then I felt
the weaving of his body next to mine.

Then I saw my father through my mother's eyes.
And he lied.

He told her we'd only stopped a while.
He'd only had a few.  He'd only had

a beer or two.
Without knowing, on that threshold  I knew
it was not beer he drank on that long stretch
of afternoon but something to pin the three of us
right where we stood.

## One Way to Remember It

I

Our mother gathers us into her Church of Outlandish
Faith: "We'll wait for Daddy" and we wait—holding
dinner, holding our breaths until the moment
life starts up again
on our exhaled and unnamed fear.

Like most nights he finally appears, transformed
from the all-out man who had left us that very morning
to the one now in the doorway, so precipitous, so drained.

The menu for the night in white chalk
on the kitchen blackboard had tricked those of us who
fell under its spell: dinner for four: mother, father, son,
daughter, the clamor of silverware and chatter.

Now the meal's particulars catch in our throats like words
or tears.

II

The grinding ride from the Lobby
to the 7th Floor is endless but hardly
long enough for smoothing his hair,
examining his nails, preparing the story
of how the guys in the office stood
a solid wall of protest against his
having to catch the bus, having to hit
the buzzer. He sees himself framed
in the doorway, the good

father, as if his hands would not tremble
for a shot, just a shot of any remedy.
Maybe just one more than one. And
as the elevator clangs its way
to the solemn gathering
at the dining room table, he jingles
his pocket change, conjuring the story
that explains how he's been missing
and what he has to offer in his place.

III

She has perched so often on the porcelain throne, looking
up, watching him lather the stubble on his craggy face.
He has peered so often into the mirror which
gives back his cragginess in spades. He attends
to his beard and hums wordless responses
to her pleas, his mouth white with lather. Scratch.
Scratch. The razor rides the rough terrain
of his sunken, or in any case, sinking cheeks.
She begs him to please come home tonight straight
from work. She recites the dinner menu and
her love for him. He nods. He hums.

The turquoise tiles
and stainless steel, the murmur
of water, her words, drown out the world.
They are locked in a kingdom so secure
no season reaches there. No child.
No priest. No dreamless sleep
until, at last, his reflection
disappears.

## Winter's Child

She no longer recalls what brought her
to that exact spot where hers was the only breath,
hers the only eyes marking the endless distance
ahead, the endless distance back. Her boots,
weighted snow casts of her feet and icy socks,
refused to rise out of their snow bound holes,
wondrous traps she'd made herself. She wonders

now what she has added to that late day storm,
the missing sun: *in their 7th floor window*
*her mother's face in an oval of steam. One by one*
*the apartment house lights twinkling on.*
*Her father, sober and home on time,*
*swooping her off the elevator, tugging off her boots,*
*laughing, rubbing her feet and hands warm.*

## Three Days

*for my father*

I

Above your hospital bed the TV stares us down,
a dumb, mounted beast. The only noise
in such a narrow room, my own small turns.
Shaking out your robe. Making sure you have
your aftershave. Change for the paper. There.
Until I am stalled, my hands on the railing
that separates your pain from mine.

II

Through the safety rail
you hold out each hand,
thin as the sticks Hansel used
to fool the Witch.
Your nails, brittle and long,
shatter ahead of my scissor blades.
You say you are ashamed.

III

Your room has become impossible
to navigate, rigged with dangerous air
and three-legged things. Just once,
side-stepping, led by a nurse, I make it back.
Together we change your bed, guiding you
through her tricky maze of sheets.

Between our strength
your body came and went.

## When All She Can Do Is Not Enough

*Mary, mother of us, where is your relief?*
– Gerard Manly Hopkins

No fall is steeper than the fall that starts
with birth. Still, what do we know of it—
our first steps, the ground so close we
bounce back before we can fathom
danger or better yet, we are swept
up by a mother right in back of us who,
mindful of the risk we take, stands
unwilling to let us fall without her ladder
of love to scamper up.

Ah, we surmise, assuming our
missteps go right, a fall is not so
treacherous after all, and blind
to the fatal cliff ahead we sally forth
like fools, it must be said, forgetting
death carves a cliff without a mother
hovering there, vigilant and perfect
in her delivery of us from birth to
everlastingness.

## When Less Than Perfect Is Enough

On the day we drove all the way to Jones Beach,
Parking Lot 11, the day no one thought to lure me
from the Atlantic's perfect waves, twice my
10-year-old height and a million, trillion times

my weight, the day the sun etched freckles
to map the me not covered up and, not content
with that, burrowed past my pale defense with heat
whose ripening evidence arose only on the long trip

to my bed, past ten packed parking lots, over
the Whitestone Bridge and the Bronx River Parkway, up
the 7 floors to the dead white sheets you encased me in,

sticky with the Noxema you slathered on my misery—
by my bed that day, the next and the next, you hovered over me,
perfect love the remedy for imperfect mothering.

## Going Away

The paper lining of the trunk my mother packed
for my yearly stay at sleep-away camp was browned
and peeling from its wooden space, more
like autumn's ruin than summer's bright start.

The open trunk took in light and air along
with my tee shirts and camping gear but
gave back a smell just like Mrs. Witty's
down the hall from our Bronx apartment—

of furniture somehow kept safely in Latvia
throughout World War II. My mother and I watered
her plants the winter she made a return visit
to that distant place with the husband who was

her deceased husband's brother because that's
what family loyalty asks one to do.
My mother and I went from room to
room, dwarfed by the chests and cabinets

that gleamed with secrets laden
with unwanted gloom and the smell
of locked rooms whose doors had withstood
violence and storms. My mother lifted

the seat of Mrs. Witty's piano bench and
chose music sheets as easily as plucking
wildflowers without names or pedigree
and played ... Mozart I think. Or sometimes

Chopin brings me to believe
that was the music she played that day,
the first I ever knew my mother could
unravel the mystery of notes and keys

and music capable of holding a world at war,
the Wittys and me, at Little Flower Camp,
homesick for my mother's back, so straight
before the waiting piano.

## Where the Ocean Begins

*for my sons*

You swim at night, scooping stars
from the water's steeliness or
by day, fracturing sunlight, oblivious
to the heat it gives you anyway.

And yet, when I ask if you can hear
the ocean's ebb and flow in shells'
corridors, you admonish me for such
foolishness. Don't I know we only conjure up

the shells' once roiling bed? Maybe so,
but I do know that ocean is everywhere,
starting when you were the fish and I
the safe haven, dense and brackish.

The sea undulates, teaching us the rhythm.
Your children, some yet unborn, dance along
the beach's edge, each at once seagull,
amphibian, fish, briny depths

and the depth's waves, hard-earned
and then gone. But the children return.
Perhaps not the same children, but then,
see how the ocean begins again.

## Topography Lesson

*for Keith Sexton*

The night I took you
to see the moon—mother and son,
we stood between the ice-shorn marsh
and the Sound.

With no rooted thing to hide the face
you said you had never—and all of fourteen—
been able to find, here the moon
sought you out.

To match the shadowed spots my finger marked
the moon's, you struck your chin at 5 o'clock,
lined up your eyes at 10 and 2.
Plains and craters mirrored then,

you recognized what you had always known.
The sweet joke of your unlikely height
and weight leaning into mine, we finally turned,
our walk across the snow-bound sand

ruffling the silence
no lovers sought that night.

## Night Lights

You were the last to hear
how a man bearing shadows
snared from the moon entered your house
after you slept, your daughter's fair hair
let down to draw him in. Or, with her hair wound
at the nape of her neck, how she opened
the back door. How he
shut out the moon.

By day, you had not guessed the difference,
the significance of the sleep she could not
cast off. Now that you've told her what you know,
she laughs at such an imaginative tale. Offers
her bobbed hair as evidence. And though
she has won your kiss goodnight,
under the window of your dreams
her uncertain light moves by.

## Around We Go

*for Michael Sean*

I think of the times I wanted to grind your foot
beneath a polite, quiet table. Or, when I could haul
you around, how often I'd have to leave the room,
your fussing more than a mother could forestall

with kisses or a breast's sweet offering. Such a sour start
for a boy whose eyebrows arched like angel's wings,
my motherliness poor match for nights sleepless from cries
no rightful angel would let loose!

So just when did you earn those angel wings? Well,
maybe not, but close enough to fly this house and settle
in a house with two prickly angels of your own.

Enough to maintain, without a thought, that you'd
want to die before life flies from either of your winged girls.

## Miss Maddie at Thirteen Takes Up the Offer to Ride in the Front Seat and Never Looks Back

Our granddaughter launches
pell-mell into her recent week
in California, including everything,
everything delicious she ate at
Grandma Pie's, the real baker,
the counterpart to me—I who at most
dice and chop, write poetry
and forget kids have to eat. Who
from my back seat seek and find Miss Maddie
framed in the side view mirror
of our cranky Escape, her careless hair
half-secured above the broad sweep
of her uncomplicated brow,
her mouth constant and sweet
with chatter that hearkens
back and then to some
grand advance and back again,
Vermont's evergreens flying past her
flying hair, until I am no longer
sitting where I sit, her grandfather
no longer in the driver's seat.

## Listening In

In the locker room a mother
and small-voiced daughter enter
adjoining showers.  I hear
their voices rise above their
twin cascades.  Hear the ping

on the metal divider between
their matching work to remove
this morning's ocean salt and all
of the beach that clings. The daughter
calls out to let her mother know

she was able to reach the soap.
To let her know how the water
helps her rinse off all the soap.
All by herself.
She inquires if her mother likes

her shower too and her mother
laughs an answer which flows
above, below the divider to reach
the child's upturned face.
Her soapy feet.

I have had only sons and never
minded until this steamy room.
Not a longing, really, but a blossoming
a mother and daughter happened
to include me in.

## Having Suggested a Reunion with My Son and Assuming His Silence Meant We'd Meet, August 15, 10 A.M.

*for Richard Lawrence*

Replacing the heat shimmering
over the road with its own heat,
its weight pressing the asphalt
into a denser, marked black,
your car, slowed for the turn,
will alter the landscape
any minute.

From the highway's thousand possibilities
I discount only those hauling wood or kids
leaning from windows. Or those
whose plates are the colors of Texas,
Vermont, New Mexico…

Although how do I know you
haven't crossed the borders of this state?

*You've moved to a mountain ledge*
*or seaside house on sticks.*

*You've settled into life*
*on a farm. Wind lifts my letter*
        *from field*
    *to field.*

*You've borrowed a van*
*from a friend back East for the visit,*
*side windows full of stickers.  A hauler*
*of wood and kids.*

Every mix of steel and glass suggests
something I might have forgotten.
Something I should have guessed.

This one.   This one.   This one.
This one will break from the traffic's hold.

*You move onto this road's narrow heat*
*in a vague white machine.*
*Or in a behemoth truck with silver stacks.*
*You clamber down its silver steps*
*to find me in my new striped cotton dress,*
*my handbag full of photographs.*

TESTIMONY

## What It Took to Wake Up

It might have come too late to be considered by most
good luck but there it was: a railroad apartment on 89th
between First and York and a job with the City of New York
for $5040 a year. Add to that having Harvey Tischler

in my D.S.S. Unit, gay as paint, who taught me by example the art
of saying *fuck* right in the middle of a sentence. Right
in the middle of every sentence. And hearing him I awoke
from a year of sorrow-induced sleep in which no life

stirred other than the quickening life I carried to term
and promptly surrendered with all the right prompting.
What could stir me from the trance of a mother gone amiss?
Nothing until Harvey blew in our door every work day,

noting how every fucking thing was wrong and how the fuck
was he supposed to get going? And I said "How the fuck is right."

## Testimony

I am tempted to point out what I tell you
is the truth but then you should know this
by the words lined up like a poem's words,
inherently as true as the hard breath after a race.
As absolute as the refusal to believe god exists.

All this to say I don't remember if we kissed.
He called me into the bed I'd let him have
in my walk-up on Avenue A and Third. He lived
with me, you see, when he wasn't on the road
with his band and his bass. I had said, "Sure,

stay here," because he wasn't Union
and sometimes wasn't paid for a gig so
of course I loved him for being thin and
smoking weed and because friends thought
I looked like him. And I remember the strangeness

of coming to a man for the first time.
Not unlike the ocean's roll toward the beach
under the moon, I rolled toward him, dreamy as water,
and turbulent, and barely knew kisses
or the bed's confines or the morning shore.

## This Spring

*in memory of K.B.M.*

I've composed the bulk
of this missive in my head,
walking the beach at exactly
the time of year we used
to get together at Marie's.

Remember hanging out
on her cottage deck? How
we'd let our conversation
drop, the drone of the waves
centering us?

And where are you now,
my friend? In the beak of a tern.
In the stem or leaf of some weedy thing.
Perhaps settled polished filigree
on the bottom of the Chesapeake.

June and the water is still freezing
here in Long Island Sound.
Remember what we called a swim,
ducking and screaming as soon
as our lungs rebounded from the shock

of being packed in ice? Well, OK. Not quite.
And remember how you and I settled
on the sheltered deck, our lives tottering
on either side of that moment, so salty
and perfectly wet?

## Palm trees, notwithstanding

the torrential rain they failed to
hold above our huddled selves

romance me yet.

No trip south is without
desire rekindled.  My aunt

from whom I lied my way
into the raging night

is dead.  Long dead.

Still, her complicated glance
peers beneath every tree

with something that seems

like forgiveness.  She knew
he waited down the street.

Or so it seemed when I

returned in disarray.
Drenched.  Smiling.

When she pretended to sleep.

## Not the Right Time for God or Country

His body hung from the trunk of his neck like a block
of cement.

My dream of a man was esoteric, poetic-
ally thin and languorous.
                                        What was I doing with this

rectangular man still snagged in jungle undergrowth? What
with this camouflaged man who should have known it was
too hot for quenching my thirst with laced punch. Who should
have said…

oh I don't know…

            *Watch out, little one, for the dangerous*
*mix of spirits with summer's lack of forgiveness.*

                    who should have said…   *Come out-*
*side with me under this sky-laden night to follow the stars*
*it lets fly*            Instead I

passed out
and he poured me into the front seat
of his waiting tank.            His weight

was enormous and damp and I hissed in his ear
what now seems ridiculous:

"If you want me you'll have to remove the Miraculous Medal
from around my neck"
and his laughter
collapsed the muscle and bone of his intent.

He must have driven me home without a word
about how he'd like to see me again, and I've since
learned to carry on without knowing
one Marine or calling on religion to save me.

## When Gratitude Trumps Regret

*"Just stop lying about yourself and kidding yourself about tomorrows."*
– Hickey in "The Iceman Cometh"

It took more than the pint of Rye and two low ball glasses
he stashed in his bottom drawer for the Irish likes of me
to win me over.

More, in fact, than the Shakespeare he rattled off for some
sought emphasis, his rhetorical point
sharpened and gentled at once.

More than his take on the vicissitudes of telling the truth
he paraded onto his Professorial stage in the guise of Hickey,
that purveyor of truth who knocked so many he sought to save dead.

More than his blindness which, despite a center which
would not hold, found and held you in his practiced periphery:
nowhere to fall/nowhere to go.

Truth was, I was all his that day of our last conference
before commencement into some vaguer world, when
he rummaged up the pint and two glasses for our final

round and I said, "Let's plan to get together, let's
have lunch ..." (Might I have said, "Let's dance"?) and he
put down his glass, searched and found me, and said,
*No.*

Goodbye was no more, no less. Next year, and every year
new students would arrive. Some with whom, I imagine,
he would have a drink. Some perhaps a smoke.

And they would need him then, to listen
with his unsullied attention, to set each one of them
on the sharp edge of his perfect vision.

## What Seemed Then Like Love

I. Abstinence

Look, I'm sorry I didn't smoke last night,
virtue clamped to my mouth like a vice,
my voice restrained by the need to
Breathe Deep. To scaffold myself
with phrases kept beneath my ribs
with rivets of air. Pure air. Interior
pink as an unwrapped gift
secured by my heart's clear stone.
I should have smoked and blown blue
love around you in rings.

II. Seascapes

We should have sailed to watch
the whales, their huge fluttering
against the sea. Ridden their descent,
our heads pressed against their singing.
Instead, the sea-embroidered edge
of our white, white sheet
above your shoulder's crest
carried me.

III. Where We Are Always Going

Now we have settled
our car, our cardboard

trunks lined with dried flowers—
gypsies, with our life lines
clutched against the wheel,
gold rings catching
the road's light and shadow.
Leaves design our hours,
green and weighted
with heaven's small songs.
We hum and pretend
we have come home.

IV. Strong Words

You have said we'll walk
the forest when the leaves have turned
further from their green, when sun
and wind set our narrow path
afire in the cold. And though
autumn rain has robbed the woods
of light and left every leaf brown
and sodden underfoot, I'll hold
your promise against the threat
of early frost, against
the last leaves' dark
and starless forms.

V. Coming to Terms

We've come to live
with unfinished business,
the room we've chosen

too small to unpack our crates
of nameless things,
our nightstand cluttered
with useless keys.
Behind us nothing
but the constant ocean
of our coming going.
We thread together our history.
Wetting our fingers, we set
its knots to our teeth,
securing our small domain.

## VI. Predictions

I have talked of sadness as if
it were all we own,
of the early darkness of autumn.
You have sat by the window
of our countless rooms, measuring
each scene with precision, noting
the moon, its patterning. Counting
the swans leaving. Predicting
their return.
And you have turned to me again
and again, insisting on sun
piercing winter's steel dome.
On the hope in rain.

## VII. Quest

If I have looked for god
in your eyes, that was a mistake.

Not that you don't hold grace
like a sweet trap. Not
that I haven't ridden
time's broom across
the crescent of your face.
I have seen the start
of the Universe, its explosion-
rocking dreams
every 4 a.m. Again
and again I've trembled forth
creation, sleep
be damned.

VIII. Surviving

Explorers, you and I have known
the danger signs all along,
memorizing our bodies' terrain,
tracking the storm. It was no accident
we came upon this room. Now we try

to leave nothing undone.
In the hall we estimate is east
I've lit the ceiling light.
Through our half-closed door,
we mark our distance
from the Universe.

West, you've rigged our one-way radio
for weather. News of the storm
blows toward our bed, its ice edge
eased by old songs, the voices
of lonely callers. Still,

we understand the night
is full of rage.  To ward off
the madness that can come
to such a cut-off place, we fold
and unfold the day's intermittent dreams,
whispering into the small warmth
we remembered to bring.

In shadows settled as stone
snow buries our well-earned sleep,
our incandescent moon burning on.

## IX. Constants

Midnight drops its moon and stars
down the sky's black clock,
the staid horizon certain
to gather the dark.  To give back
the light.  And I, my love, circle
the earth's steady spin,
waiting for morning
and your uncertain return.

## On Not Remembering Just When Love Died

Take the love that had set you smoking again.
The love that took your eyes off the road, your car
lost in a series of drifts into cars ahead, red lights a signal,
not to stop but to dream instead, of that very night

in an endless stretch of endless nights you'd smoke
and love so well you'd forget to eat or remembering,
have no appetite left.

You'd never imagined then, one day your eye would heed
the red light's Stop, your foot find the brake.
That a bit of toast would reawake your love to eat.

Today you're not sure just which night failed
to materialize. Just which night you propped yourself
against your own bolster in your own bed,
smoking a last cigarette.

## Driving Home

With no time for a contrived message,
no love call across the white line, the speed
no sweet bed for idleness, a shared cigarette,

you signal with a smile,
a hint our exits may be the same.
An invitation to the dance
in the back room of a place
I too have dreamed.

I signal back and along the asphalt loom
we weave a remnant of the afternoon:
we pass each other, smile and pass again

until I want to roll the window down and shout
*All right!* To run you off the road,
our wheels locked, fenders sparked.
On the slopes of the soft shoulder
I want to inspect the gear loaded on your truck

but our smiles are stuck behind the glass
and steel we each have locked. Darkness
rides the oncoming miles.

On an uphill stretch I pull ahead, cross
to the lane you're not allowed.
In my rear-view mirror I watch for you,
watch for you,
          watch for you ...

## Trips

When you go away on business
or some other pressing matter
like your mother's insistence,
I plan to take the locks off
all the windows you shut each night
to keep us safe from sorrow
and the loss of our silver.

The moment I calculate the wheels
of your craft are tucked up
useless spheres,
I will run from lock to lock,
slamming their half-moons out,
forcing each window its height.

I have dreamed of being blown
across the room, of suffering
the vapors.
At night I will be tickled
by the fear of thieves.
I gage that when your wheels
hit ground again, I will have been stolen,
your children gobbled up.

## At Summer's End

Their conversation is of everyday stuff,
wondering when they should stop mowing
the lawn. Wondering how long to allow

for their trip south. Wondering when
to close up the house.
And wondering if their three sons

in three places are roaming under the same sun
that's dazzling this bay and wondering if they're not
overcome by its brazenness.

Or does that wondering actually come later on,
as the sun's shadows steal the day? Oh, of course,
it isn't the sun's shadows but all the objects in its way:

the still leafed weeping willow, the billowy field
of marsh grass, their own car making its way home.
He drives and she lets sun and shadow

cross her drowsiness. She thinks of how
he had stopped ahead of her at the overlook
and how long it seemed before he turned back.

BREAKING NEWS

## A Test for Poetry's Capacity to Engender Change

*Art enables us to find ourselves and lose ourselves at the same time.*
— Thomas Merton

Pick up the pencil.
No, no. Like this,
the point toward the paper.
That's it.

Write what you recall of the accident.
Words forced through lead have a cathartic effect
in cases like yours. Tears are essential, of course,
but in the matter of a husband and two sons, barely enough.

Haven't you observed how tears
slip through your fingers, your palms
as catch basins, useless? Written words,
conversely, hold their own.

Now. Now. That's it.
Write your name. The name of your husband.
Your two sons. Excellent! These symbols will allow you
to trace your recollections, the smallest regrets.

Experiment with their order. Note the change
in rhythm with their change in order. Remove
one name, then another. Write a sentence.
Note how it leads to a stanza, how it calls for forgiveness.

Soon you will stop wringing your hands,
wiping them on your skirt. One hand will hold the pencil,

one the paper at a perfect slant.  There, inclined
toward your sorrow, metaphors lead to myth.

If our predictions are correct, within a month
the lost toy found under your bed,
the collar stay at the back of a drawer
will only serve to vitalize your art.

## Tintype

The baby stares dead ahead,
its dumpling hands arranged
against the pleated skirt spread
across its lap. Nothing makes it laugh.

Not the man with the powder puff
we guess, bent low to dust its gray
temples with light then lift
the single row of lace higher on its neck.

Nor the mother who hovered
close by, her own hands useless.
She knew no craft could quicken the child
she had heard cry only the day before.

We can picture her though,
holding this cold likeness to her lips.
Whispering.
Insistent it take her breath.

## A Season of Rain

*The day returns, but nevermore*
*Returns the traveler to the shore.*
– Henry Wadsworth Longfellow

On your long ride home your Focus
leaves a wake of rising rain,
road after flooded road.

Behind your house you find the salt marsh
has disappeared beneath a lake
that's rising with the rain and run-off
and the moon's attraction, despite
its light's long absence.

Or perhaps the moon
is permanently gone, like your brother
who one night took a last, wild drive
beyond the firmament.

Or your boys who at childhood's every turn
left you to wonder where the children had gone.
By what trick of time they had turned into men.

Or yourself, no longer yesterday's you.

Not even who you were the last half-
hour at your kitchen sink. The you who stared
out over the reedy lake behind your house and dreamed
the rain would never stop. Who dreamed it was you
who would sleep tonight and rise tomorrow.

## Midnight Call

Our stop and go advance
toward the rolled-over van is
wordless. Breathless. Until

we see them climb
from the upended doors,
one by one, dazed but
smiling. Happy
(if happiness travels
this close to death)
for their wobbly legs,
their hungry lungs,
the wind's snowy persistence.

And seeing the survivors' array
of ski hats and bright mittens rising
into the storm's white advance,
we reach for our coffee.
We breathe. We are gone.

Not that all walk away.
My brother, for one.
Shifting
to the opposing lane
just as the oncoming car
crossed the line.

The moment they both
caught their mistake.
Their attempt to return...

Not that I know
that night. That road.

I barely know (as one
might know
a hard-earned truth)
the call that, strangely,
came to me. His sister. Only
his sister. Who knows
how the call skirted
his wife? Skirted our mother.

His boys, now, are grown.
They don't know I got that call.
But when I see them, I hear
the phone ring. I turn
to the wall and try
to return to sleep.

In the only dream
to which I cling
past bed, past
morning,
my sons and
my brother's sons
emerge from doors
dazed and smiling.
Bright notes
in white-out storms.

## Wasted

*for Mike*

Had any of us seen through
your letter, October 21, 1976,
signed with aplomb and no hint
of regret, to the local police

with copies to the mayor and
Fort Lauderdale Press,
thanking them for their
steadiness in extracting you

from your motor vehicle
and delivering you home
to your loving wife and
adoring sons who,

you were sure, would be
eternally grateful, we might
have been forearmed. But
nothing changed and eternity

proved ephemeral between
the crumpled hood
and sullen door
of that rescued night

and November 14, 1979
when no sirens wailed

right to the mark you'd have
thought they would,

no cops on the spot
to prop you smartly beside
your deadly wreck.
No cops to brush you off.

To say, "It's OK, fella.
We'll have you home
before your family knows
just how late it is."

## One or Two Crows and So On

1

The crow, alight on this sawed-off pole,
despite his darkness, his dismal caw,
his barely elevated perch, points as skyward
as a missile ought, with no thought
of heaven but regardless, heading there.

2

Lucretius, despite the absence of Enlighten-
ment, knew atoms explained the whole of us,
our humble flesh and bones no less stars
than all those that light the firmament.

3

When my brother's flesh and bones
gave up their light on Interstate 95,
I followed his trajectory to the sky, sure
he'd landed among the stars. He's there
nights, and even days, when we are blind to stars.

4

What's more, branches mirrored
in the stilled stream glimmer,
the thin light above the woods just
enough to lend itself to the otherwise
winter-dark water.

5

My thoughts are earth-bound now,
atoms here enough distraction
from what might have been heaven.

6

One husband, three sons, two
daughters-in-law, a third
dwelling in the wings of possibility,
five granddaughters, one grandson,
two nephews, thirty-odd
face-to-face friends, three cousins,
seven cousins once-removed and,
out of the original ten, one aunt
alive in the Catskills.

7

Aunt Annabelle lives alone.
We've yet to fly to her.
Poke. Poke.

8

One crow still sits.
One crow sits still.

9

The crescent moon's the knocker
on Heaven's Door. I find myself
knocking there now and then, say,
on my drive home, the moon's door
swinging open on some forgotten thought.
Some relocated loss.

10

Cell phone.
Landline.
iPad
laptop
Skype.
Son.
Granddaughter.
Grandson. And
so on.

11

One crow
pokes one
crow off.
One crow flies.
One crow
points to
where he
plans to go

12

Despite your gingerly walk
up the slippery path, despite
your stolen glance to the sawed-
off pole, you find the crows
have flown.

## She's Twenty

She's twenty, only two times ten
swift years and nowhere to be found.
She seems to have forgotten

she'd kept us waiting so often
for her key's reassuring sound.
She's twenty, only two times ten.

Her stories grew from just pretend
to lies she carelessly unwound.
She seems to have forgotten

how we let our lives upend
with every lie. Unhappy clown!
She's twenty, only two times ten,

with lies in dream's disguise taken
to a man called Love. So far from home
she seems to have forgotten

we're waiting open armed. We spend
each night listening for her key's sweet turn.
She's twenty, only two times ten.
She seems to have forgotten.

## That summer afternoon the rain

multiplied by branches pulled aside
by the campers before us, splashed our limbs
and bathing suits, still wet from our swim.
(Only the counselors' whistles had revealed
the thunder's roll. Only their yells
had pulled us ashore.)

Walking brave as brave Junior Campers
we laughed and swallowed all the rain we could
until the trail's easy mud started its slide
toward the lake. Thunder broke apart the air,
the round of our thin voices. Mud swallowed
our stepping stones. Now each of us folded herself
deeper inside her towel's heavy comfort. Each
watched her own step.

Just ahead woods gave way to the trail.

In the flat gray light that seemed to ease
the rain, three Senior Girls were waiting,
hands on the deepened shelves of their hips.
Mouths pressed into that sneer of Senior Girls.

Behind me the trail was still.

"Take your bathing suit off," one of them said.
"Come on, come on, the others taunted." Over the pure
convex of my ribs I crossed my arms, yelled "Don't you dare
touch me—stay where you are or I'll scream *Rape*
and I mean it." "*Rape*," they mimicked, splattering rain,

narrowing space. "You don't even know what rape is."
"I don't care—*Rape! Rape! Rape!"* my voice pushed up
through the rain into light.

Now they looked scared. "Shut up, kid, shut up.
Get back to your cabin and not a word of this.
Prissy miss. Little shit."

Following the streams of hair matted to their faces,
water ran down their necks, onto the rise of their breasts.
Beyond them wind drove the rain from the catch basins
of leaves, onto the narrowing trail.

## Radio Triptych

Sobs drown her words
in a torrent
of grief. Grammar
eludes her.
My son. Gone.
My daughter. My
house. We hesitate

in our task
of watering flowers.
Writing a letter. Matching
socks. Into the frame
of geography
the reporter sets
the scene. Oh, there.

Mogadishu. Gaza.
New Orleans. We sigh.
Of course. We try to decipher
the background sounds.
The drone of a plane.
An animal scratching.
The crush of stone.

## A Measure of Safety

*in Kabul, Hama, Damascus...*

I know the map of this kitchen.
How many paces from its south wall
to its north, how many east to west.

I know the measure of its sugar
and salt. The measure of oil
I gauge by its weight.

I know, from its window, the point
our street vanishes into the rubble
of our neighborhood. A street that once
had no vanishing point.

I know the breathing of our children
asleep in the next room. Their
whimpering sleep.

Awake, my children imagine I know
how to keep them safe. In dreams,
danger seeps through every measured wall.

## Breaking News, Baghdad

The idea of bread can only be
arrived at directly,

(I taste it)

basic and essential as the human
connection it connotes: the warmth

(reconnected)

the oven gives off, the whiff of love,
the wine conjured up, the pre-dawn

(only the moon / the waiting moon)

hours each baker starts, flour dust
caking his apron, a smidgen across

(a lover, a foolish lover)

his nose where his glasses slip
from the heat of his work, his oven,

(dark and certain)

his bread, slid onto its waiting rack.
But wait.  No bread today.

(The lover lies alone)

Each baker with his flour dust,
his moonlit enterprise that seemed

(I taste it)

so much like love
has been dragged from his cozy shop

and...
have you heard?

(It tastes of salt)

shot.

## Together the Squirrel and I

Together the squirrel and I registered our horror.
Although it was I who was safe on the sidewalk,
my height providing the right perspective.
The wheel and the squirrel were perfectly aligned.

No irreducible space would save him.
But at the time that wasn't absolutely certain
to either one of us. Together we raised up
our paws / hands to ward off
the oncoming weight. I forgot myself
and yelled, "Stop! Dear god oh my god stop!"

But my supplications were no more heard
than the squirrel's. His front paws joined,
his face lifted up, he died
and by the second wheel died a second time.

So his life ended, although not the accident
that was left of him. Even as I watched
more cars came. One only close.
Its wake lifted his tail,
then let it drop. So much for hope.

For days I was half-dead myself,
the vision of fragile life gone
raw on my brain.
But I was also half alive,
having a good old alive time.
It had been, after all, the squirrel.

And passing by the spot later in the week
I saw he had been reduced to a small,
dense rise the color of tar.
It seems even in these modern times
nature accommodates us all.

## Adjacent Places

I once had neighbors whose uncle lived with them.
They said, for some reason, they owed it to him.
Still, it seemed extraordinarily generous,
an old man like that, expecting his lunch on time,
his nodding silence.

Throughout the warmer months he sat
the farthest distance from their house
in an arbor that separated their lot
from mine. I could make out his shadow
in the shadow of trees,
that responsibility, bald and crooked,
bent over what seemed a consuming task.

"He is copying," my friends explained,
"cross-word puzzles from used books"—
the grids, the clues, down and across.
Copying their unlikely solutions.

"Well, work is man's dignity," I said.
We giggled. We agreed.

Certain days in autumn
remind me of those huddled trees.
I imagine their leaves' descent.
The waiting ground.
The redwood bench.

## Some Homely Advice on Buying a House

after the Real Estate Section, *The New York Times*

Give up thoughts of living
rooms, the arrangement of things like seasons,
sun and moon circling the house you dream:
next center of the universe. We would suggest

no house is safe for dreams. Door frames bruise.
Oak trees darken the baby's room. Bread burns.
Seasons re-route air, the traffic pattern. Your family
and friends are caught in storms. Windows jam.

You can't get out. Measure instead, the progress of light
across the room to the bed where you'll be propped, every pillow
in the house plumped against your death. Bedside,
the obligatory glass of viscous cure, abandoned as useless.

Visitors pass in ante-rooms, clucking the shame of it, words
drowned in held-back tears. Your own tears held bravely
in a handkerchief. Down the hall your child comes heel-to-toe
carrying tea. In the study the doctor and your spouse

no longer speak. Head tilted
toward that unfamiliar quiet, imagine each room
in the narrowing light. In the darkness that follows
choose a house.

## A House Close to the Ground

*for Bob Lorenz*

When he was done every room in the house hugged the ground
and every window framed the flowers he'd planted one by one,
a patch of sky, a tree limb with a bird feeder waiting for birds
that were sure to come to feed and look in on her who looked
out room-to-room to see all she had lost easy access to
and the birds flew down and sang and flew off again and sun
and rain, sun and rain marked off the days, and the seasons flew
and he brought her tea and slipped her feet into her slippers
and brought bouquets of flowers in when she
became too tired to look out any window in any room.

## Redefinition

It may be disingenuous to call this happiness, but the man
with his mountain of black plastic bags overflowing with
all he's known, rag by rag—a scarf, a gown, yesterday's news
and all the days' before, bright metal stuff

or stuff that's turned—calls for some kind of summing up.
From the one subway seat upon which he sits,
his bags cascade into black valleys,
seats west, seats east.

Out of the mountain's settled top he extracts an arm
to fan himself with half an envelope, small treasure
from the shiny universe he not only created but oversees
in its own gently rocking orbit.

## Another Story

*for Amy*

We're four abreast in the darkened theater.
I didn't want to go to this girlie movie
but I reserve my discerning scorn

for another time, away from these friends
of mine, all from our support group for,
excuse the expression, cancer survivors.

Truth is, some of us are surviving
better than the rest. One in our little band,
Amy, is swathed in too many clothes

for this June day, her head topped
with a woolly knit cap. If we want to forget
what's up, her scarf and cap

refuse to let us off their dreadful hook:
signs that treatments, even as they're given,
might only make you sick.

For two hours plus we sit as one,
watching four 40-Somethings
fling themselves at life like life is theirs,

notwithstanding insubstantial men and
occasional flops. Not so unlike us.
At least the flinging part. To credits

and an upbeat score, we file out
into the post-matinée light.  Holding on
to what we've got.  A few good friends.  A few

good laughs.  And a day that started out
rainy that's brightened up.  Not sunny exactly,
but something close to what we want.

## Dedication

*for John*

Now and then I look up
and find you across the room,
reading, maybe, or on the phone.

And, although never seeming
to be lost in a dream, you appear
to me not unlike a dream,

your hazel eyes and Irish blush
suddenly *Here*, as if
I'd failed to see you all along:

your funniness, your willingness
to listen, to read a poem of mine
out loud so it arrives

unexpectedly, a poem as fresh
as one drifting from a meadow
or over an ocean.

# About the Author

Pat O'Brien has written poetry for as long as she can remember, and poetry has been an essential tool in exploring and expressing her relationship to her family of origin, to her nuclear family, to her place in the world with all its richness and all its upheavals, and to her field work as a licensed social worker. In the latter capacity, she has worked with under-served populations in New York City and Bridgeport, and with those in medical crisis or affected by adoption. She has also helped to establish and maintain Hospice services in three Connecticut prisons, including the York Correctional Institute for Women, where she brought poets, artists, and other professionals to work with Hospice inmate volunteers and staff.

After completing her Social Work degree at Columbia University, Pat was lucky enough to attend literature and poetry classes taught by oustanding teachers including Dick Allen, Peter Ulysse, Don Barkin, Maggie Nelson, Patricia Klindienst, and Edwina Trentham. She has been an active member of Guilford Poets Guild and more recently helped to co-found Connecticut River Poets. Her fellow poets in these groups have been invaluable in broadening her understanding of poetry and helping her nudge her own work into shape.

Her work has appeared in many journals including *Poet Lore, Connecticut River Review, Embers, Pulp Smith, Connecticut Library Journal, Fresh Water,* and *Connecticut Review.* It has also received awards from the Trumbull Arts Council, Acton Public Library, and *Embers* magazine.

For over 20 years Pat has been assimilating the valuable teachings of the Shambhala/Buddhist tradition, learning to practice two of its vital principles: *Don't be attached to an outcome* and *Be open to all possibilities.*

She resides in Old Saybrook with her husband, John, and not too far from their three sons, Richard, Michael, and Keith, their amazing partners, and their terrific kids, six in all.

This book is set in Garamond Premier Pro, which had its genesis in 1988 when type-designer Robert Slimbach visited the Plantin-Moretus Museum in Antwerp, Belgium, to study its collection of Claude Garamond's metal punches and typefaces. During the mid-fifteen hundreds, Garamond—a Parisian punch-cutter—produced a refined array of book types that combined an unprecedented degree of balance and elegance, for centuries standing as the pinnacle of beauty and practicality in type-founding. Slimbach has created an entirely new interpretation based on Garamond's designs and on comparable italics cut by Robert Granjon, Garamond's contemporary.

To order additional copies of this book
or other Antrim House titles, contact the publisher at

Antrim House
21 Goodrich Rd., Simsbury, CT 06070
860.217.0023, AntrimHouse@comcast.net
or the house website (www.AntrimHouseBooks.com).

•

On the house website
in addition to information on books
you will find sample poems, upcoming events,
and a "seminar room" featuring supplemental biography,
notes, images, poems, reviews, and
writing suggestions.